João Figueiredo

HOW DO
WE LEARN?

A GUIDE FOR MUSIC STUDENTS, TEACHERS AND PARENTS

REVISED & EXPANDED

INCLUDES 2 NEW CHAPTERS!

JF EDUCATION LTD

To Luis, my son, for you
are the reason why I do
what I do.

I love you.

How Do We Learn?

Table Of Contents:

ABOUT JOÃO FIGUEIREDO

João Figueiredo is a renowned educator, author and coach. Originally from Lisbon, Portugal, João has travelled all over the world helping students of all ages and styles.

At the age of 30, João Figueiredo has taught over 700 students in Europe, Asia and United Kingdom.

João studied and studies with some of the best drummers in the world - Claus Hessler, Juan Carlito Mendoza, JP Bouvet, Hugo Danin and Michael Lauren (co-founder of the Drummers Collective in New York City, USA) are just some of the names that have taught João over the past 15 years. João also has a degree in Sound Engineering and studied with some of the best composers and conductors in the world - Stephen Coker, Paul Caldwell, Paulo Lourenço and Gonçalo Lourenço for example.

João is an official **Soultone** USA artist, a **Drumeo** Certified Instructor, a **Vic Firth** Artist & Educator, a member of the **Sabian Education Network**, of the **D'Addario/Evans Education Collective** and a member of the **Leeds Music Education Partners**.

Obsessed with teaching and being the eternal student himself, João loves to guide and to help students finding their voices on the drum kit and to help everyone living a richer life! Being a drum teacher is his passion and drumming is just an excuse to teach.

Besides being the founder of the Leeds Drum Academy, João Figueiredo is also the founder of BeAProMuso.com (an online coaching agency for musicians) and the author of "How Do We Learn?", "Linear Drumming – One Step At A Time" and "How To Hide The Teaching".

WHO IS THIS BOOK FOR?

I've been teaching now for 11 years. And I know it's a "cliché", but I've learned as much as (I hope) my students. As I progressed as an educator, I started finding more and more patterns and similarities among the more than 700 students that I have taught thus far. The problem was that I couldn't figure out what these patterns meant. So what does a curious soul do? It studies. I started studying pedagogy, psychology, student's behavior, etc etc etc... The more I read, the more I recognized the patterns. So now I was on a mission to apply these new ideas I had based on all this newly acquired knowledge. The results were mind-blowing. Students were learning much faster, their self-awareness was improving day by day, their understanding of concepts was much deeper.

However... There were still some students that I couldn't get through. That's when I realized that those were the students who needed to know what I knew about psychology and the mental processes that we all go through when learning. Perhaps if they know how the brain works, they will start acting in a more productive fashion and they will finally achieve what they wish to achieve.

This book is for EVERYONE who struggles to learn, to be self-motivated, to stay focused and to everyone who wishes to be better.

This book is also for teachers who wish to understand their students better.

And, of course, this book is for all parents who want to help their children learn better and feel more fulfilled.

I wrote this book because I care. It would be easier if I didn't, but I do. And I'm on a mission to help everyone learn better. So if you, in anyway, feel that this book can be useful, then dig in.

EXCUSES, EXCUSES, EXCUSES...

If you're a music teacher, you've heard (at least some of) these. If you're a music student, you've probably used these. So here we go, my not so favorite excuses for why students don't practice:

1. **I didn't practice because I was away;**

2. **I didn't practice because I didn't have time;**

3. **I didn't practice because I lost my homework;**

4. **I didn't practice because I lost my drum sticks;**

5. **I forgot to practice;**

6. **I practiced but I left my homework at home;**

7. **I was busy;**

8. **I didn't practice because I didn't know what to do;**

9. **I practiced but I can't remember how it goes;**

Aren't these convincing? Exactly... If you've ever used one of these, shame on you, you've used one of the nine lamest excuses in the book.

The thing is, I don't actually think that you're lazy – or do I? – but I do know that students often lie to themselves and come up with these excuses not because they want to lie to their teacher, but often because they actually believe what they're saying. Right now, some of you might be thinking *"But I did lose my drumsticks! That's not an excuse!"*. Well, it is. If your lesson is on a Tuesday and you lost your drum sticks on the Friday before... you had 4 days to go get a new pair. Plus, are you honestly telling me that you couldn't practice without sticks?...

Remember this: where there's a will there's a way and the hungry ones never, NEVER, justify their mistakes. **They fix them.**

SMART

The first step to success is to build a strong mind and to define goals. And be careful when you do define your goals, they must be SMART. That stands for: **S**pecific, **M**easurable, **A**chievable, **R**elevant and **R**ealistic, and **T**imely. We will address this in depth in the "How To Practise" chapter.

THE 10,000 HOURS THEORY

A lot of people have heard of this theory: it takes 10,000 hours of practice to master something. But, is this completely true though?

The principle holds that 10,000 hours of "deliberate practice" are needed to achieve world-class level in any field. When psychologists talk about deliberate practice, they mean practicing in a way that pushes your skill set as much as possible. But here's what the author of this theory – Malcolm Gladwell - had to say back in 2014:

"There is a lot of confusion about the 10,000 rule that I talk about in Outliers. It doesn't apply to sports. And practice isn't a SUFFICIENT condition for success. I could play chess for 100 years and I'll never be a grandmaster. The point is simply that natural ability requires a huge investment of time in order to be made manifest. Unfortunately, sometimes complex ideas get oversimplified in translation."

So here's what really matters: **How** you practice. That is the single most important component when practicing. Think about this: how many musicians do you know who have been playing for 20 or more years and still, they're below average? I know that I know plenty. So remember this:

IT'S NOT WHAT NOR FOR HOW LONG, IT'S HOW.

What does that mean? It means that we need to evaluate and analyze our practice sessions AS WE PRACTISE, not only after. That is the real difference between practicing and playing. So here's another rule:

AT HOME BE THE STUDENT AND THE TEACHER.

ON STAGE BE AN ARTIST.

This is fundamental if you want to get the most out of your practice sessions. What is also fundamental is to understand that you can't have the same mindset when practicing that you have (or should have) when you're performing. Thomas Lang says this all the time: "**Never practice when you play and never play when you practice**". Simple words but so true. Quick explanation? When you practice, focus on what you can't do. When you perform, ONLY focus and use what you can do. So many "musicians" attempt to practice on stage… it's painful to watch.

HOW TO PRACTISE

THE CHECKLIST FOR SUCCESS

Most students don't get as many results as they wish – or even worse, they don't get as many results as **they think** they did – mainly because they don't know HOW to practice. And didn't we acknowledge already that it's all about the HOW? So here's a little list of what you should focus on when practicing:

- Failing To Plan Is Planning To Fail
- Set Goals
- Focus On The Process
- Know When To Practice
- Embrace The Suck
- Be The Judge, Not Just The Student:
  - Timing – practice slow and to a metronome
  - Dynamics – don't add your dynamics later
  - Precision – make sure you understand the phrase before you play it!
- Body language
- Sing It!
- KNOW WHY YOU ARE PRACTISING!

FAILING TO PLAN IS PLANNING TO FAIL…

This one is EXTREMELY important. Goals without a plan are just dreams. So how to plan a practice session? Simple: find your weaknesses. Only when you identify what you need to improve on you'll be able to start the process of planning your "workout" sessions. To identify your weakness is healthy but it can be daunting. Most students aren't capable of this mainly because their ego gets in the way. So here's a practical exercise:

> Think of your biggest weakness. Now think of your biggest strength. Say both out loud – that helps with acknowledgement – and write your weakness down on a piece of paper.
>
> **That is the title of your practice session plan.**

Let's see what a weekly plan could look like.

July 2016 – Week 2

Practice Routine | MAIN FOCUS: BASS DRUM

1. **BASS DRUM CONTROL – CONTROL PAGE – 15 MINS**
2. **READING TEXT IN 4/4 (BASS DRUM) – 15 MINS**
3. **BAIÃO INDEPENDENCE – 20 MINS**

A

BREAK (10 MINS)

4. **STICK CONTROL – FLAMS (20 MINS)**
5. **TIME KEEPING EXERCISES (15 mins)**
   a. Mute Bars
   b. 25bpm/50bpm
   c. Chip (improvisation)
6. Sight-reading (Odd-Meters) – 15 mins

B

BREAK (10 MINS)

1. **BASS DRUM CONTROL – CONTROL PAGE – 15 MINS**
2. **READING TEXT IN 4/4 (BASS DRUM) – 15 MINS**
3. **BAIÃO INDEPENDENCE – 20 MINS**

A

CONCENTRATION

PRECISION

MUSICALITY

Let's break it down: This practice routine uses an **ABA** structure. That means that we'll repeat the first section. That allows for easier and faster memorization of the concepts so use this technique whenever you work on new concepts. Also, define how much time you'll spend on each exercise and then stick to it. Time it, use your phone, set alarms… **do whatever it takes so you take control and stop practicing randomly and inconsequentially.**

Also, I find extremely helpful to take 5 to 10-minute breaks every hour or so. Even if you decide to practice for 6 hours, make sure you take 5 breaks. Why? Our brain is wired to memorize and learn when **not** under stress. Much like when you work out, the real benefits and growth come when you're not stressing your body but rather during the recovery time. The brain is no different. Push hard and then let it relax and absorb.

Finally, those three words (**CONCENTRATION, PRECISION and MUSICALITY**) are my focal points and the guidelines for my practice. I always make sure that these three concepts are always the rules that I practice by.

But here's what really matters! WHY you should practice.

SET GOALS

Goal setting is extremely useful and important. You're basically defining WHY (and WHAT FOR) you are practicing. The problem these days is that a lot of students practice for no reason. Which leads to… no practice. We'll address metacognition further into this book but for now, here's a practical exercise:

> *We already defined what your weaknesses are. Now is time to define how far you'll go to eliminate these weaknesses. Define __TWO__ goals for your biggest weakness. For example:*
>
> *Goals for July 2016:*
>
> *1) Play page 12 of the Syncopation book at 75 BPM;*
> *2) Grid accents (16th notes, heel down) at 70 BPM.*

You have to define short and long-term goals, otherwise you might find yourself playing and "half-practicing" ideas that you heard someone play, you saw on a YouTube video or even worse… your teacher told you to practice (see the irony?). But the big question should always be: WHY AM I PRACTICING THIS? And if you don't know the answer… either ask your teacher or just **don't practice it**. Unless those exercises are a fundamental part of your goal, then let's face it, they're going to be a waste of your time.

Now be careful, because if you set your goals too high you'll become demotivated and anxious. Set your goals too low and you'll be bored. Usually students either set their goals too high or they don't set goals at all. Below is a diagram that shows you how important it is to find that sweet spot when practicing:

Comfort Zone

Challenge Zone

Anxiety Zone

This "sweet spot" is pretty difficult to find but once you do, the benefits and the speed at what you'll feel yourself improving is going to be way worth the effort. Here's how I find out what my mindset is when I practice.

THE 3 MINDSETS OF PRACTICE

"How fast should I play this?"

I get asked this question all the time. And of course, I'm 100% guilty of responding using the most cliché of all answers: "Well, just find a tempo that is comfortable for you."

No. No. No. One thousand times no. This is not the right answer. So, before we get into any explanations for why this is so wrong... I'm sorry. I'm sorry if you ever heard me saying that. I want you to know that if you didn't progress fast enough after hearing those words coming out of my mouth... that's my fault.

It's about time I fix it.

Ok, so let's start from the beginning. If you're learning something new, you need to know where your limits are and then push them so you can improve. But how can you find those limits? Or better yet, how can you know exactly what it takes for you to "fail"? And I do mean "**EXACTLY**". You have to **MEASURE IT**.

There are 3 mindsets (or emotional zones) in practice – COMFORT, ANXIETY and CHALLENGE. These are indicators of states of mind during practice and they will demonstrate rather quickly how efficient you can be.

Let's break them down, one at a time.

COMFORT ZONE

Ah, a classic. This is the most talked about of all "emotional zones". The comfort zone means one thing and one thing only: it's easy. Dare I say, too easy. It's fairly easy to identify if you're practicing in your comfort zone. It feels… fun.

In all seriousness, the comfort zone is a dangerous zone to be in for multiple reasons, some of which I list below:

- It gives you a false impression of how well you are doing, for you might believe that you're progressing when you're really just not challenging enough;
- It nurtures a culture of laziness and avoidance. On one hand you are training your brain to be okay with not feeling the need to challenge itself, while on the other hand you're wiring your mind to always avoid mistakes – instead of making them and then fix them.

So keep your ego at bay and push yourself further. Leave that comfort zone. Go on. I dare you.

ANXIETY ZONE

Who hasn't felt anxious during practice? Everyone does, right? That means that you're challenging yourself, right?

Wrong.

It means that you're pushing yourself way past your limits – in a bad way – and you're telling your body that it's okay to feel tense, it's okay to feel stressed. Muscle memory doesn't apply only to motions or things that you actively do. It also applies to EVERYTHING your body repeats. That said, if you're always practicing under stress and feeling anxious, stop. You're not learning anything but how to be a nervous wreck.

CHALLENGE ZONE

Ah, the sweet spot. The **CHALLENGE ZONE** is where you want to be when you practice. It feels difficult, but not impossible. It feels challenging but you can still enjoy the process. Look, a lot of our learning gets affected by our emotions. If you are scared, you learn differently than if you're feeling confident or curious. I'm not saying that you can't learn under stress (of course you can), but I'm saying that you can't learn efficiently and effectively if your focus and interest in the outcome is clouded by fear and anxiety.

When learning a craft, the last thing you want to do is to "learn" by avoiding mistakes. No. That's a horrible habit to develop. Mistakes are fundamental and they teach you incredible lessons. The only (the only!!!) way you can learn from a failure or a mistake is by, immediately, embracing that mistake as a lesson, not as a defeat.

HOW CAN YOU FIND YOUR CHALLENGE ZONE?

There's one question that I haven't answered yet, which is "How can I find my challenge zone?". And that, my dear friend, is a very important question. The answer is pretty straight-forward – but if you fail to do this, you might end up practicing in your comfort zone (or should I say, not practicing?) or freaking out in the anxiety zone.

So, here's what you do: start by playing in your comfort zone. Ask yourself how it feels. Are you zoning out? Are you not making any mistakes? Are you "over-confident"? Ok, then it's time to level up. Play it faster (or add more elements, such as dynamics), and ask the same question again. Keep pushing… until it snaps. As soon as you feel that your focus had to increase for you to keep up with the speed or even just to make sure that the overall sound of the exercise isn't compromised, then you are in. That's your **CHALLENGE ZONE**.

What to do now? Well, now you practice until that tempo is again comfortable. Then you push again until you feel the same. By doing so, you don't waste time practicing to slowly or to fast and you always practice in the right mindset and state of mind. You want to feel challenged, not threatened.

16

FOCUS ON THE PROCESS

This is a difficult one. In order to focus on your practice and the process of practicing, you'll have to be in love with it. If all you care about is the end goal, then I can assure you that you'll give up before getting there. If the climb, the struggle, the challenge doesn't motivate you, then I'm afraid you won't be excited about practicing, which will lead to not achieving your goals.

Your practice session must be an on-going process of self-evaluation. If you're practicing your technique while looking at the ceiling, forget it, you won't improve. If you're working on your sound while playing along to your favorite songs, forget it, it won't happen. If instead of counting out loud you consciously decide to count in your head – or not even – then you just made the decision of slowing down your progress. You must focus on the process, you must constantly question your execution and commitment. It's perfectly normal to get bored. But to become a musician you must power through that and become focused and goal-oriented. Any other approach might end up tasting like regret…

KNOW WHEN TO PRACTICE

This is more important than what you might think. Some of us function better in the morning, some of us function better at night. Some of us write better at night but we read better after lunch. It depends on how we are wired to behave and how our metabolism works. It is quite important to find your "production schedule", for this might be one of the missing pieces of your puzzle. What if you're practicing at a time of the day that is much harder for you to absorb information? What if you're missing out on a fully immersive learning experience?

EMBRACE THE SUCK (AND BE HONEST!)

Mike Johnston[1] made this expression famous in the drumming world but this military saying is as much of a cliché as it is a necessary mindset that will allow you to power through the challenges and the difficulties. You will struggle but a strong mind will always help you in times of struggle. If you have the tendency to go short on motivation whenever you're "battling" an exercise, then here are a couple of suggestions/affirmations:

- Remind yourself of why you're practicing;
- Remind yourself of all those times when you struggled with exercises that are now natural to you and you use all the time;
- Take a break, go for a 5-minute walk and then come back;
- If you're really stuck and you seem to be out of motivation, then book a drum lesson with a great teacher nearby or via Skype. Sometimes all we need is a "kick in the bottom" and inspiration from someone who you look up to. If you already have a teacher, then open up to him/her, speak your mind and ask for guidance.

Now, it's very important that you're honest with yourself. What a lot of students lack is honesty and self-awareness – we'll discuss the latter further into this book – and those are the two elements that can make or break your practice sessions (and your future in the music business). So for example: when you're practicing say, double stroke rolls, make sure that you look for all inconsistencies – and there will be inconsistencies! – and always, ALWAYS, question your performance and take notes so you can fix it.

---

[1] Mike Jonhston is the founder of Mikeslessons.com, an online drum lessons website.

BE THE JUDGE, NOT JUST THE STUDENT

We will go deep into this subject in the next chapter, but being your own teacher and judge is fundamental in order to develop a real and strong foundation. If all you do is follow orders with no critical thinking supporting your tasks and homework, then you'll find yourself not knowing what to fix and improve. Please, do yourselves a favor and practice with one simple goal: **to become better**.

BODY LANGUAGE

Tension is perfectly normal – and needed! – but it's important to achieve balance and find the sweet spot between tension and release. In order to understand how effective your technique and motions are you'll need to watch your body language. The good news is, nowadays this is incredibly easy. If you have a smartphone… you also have a video camera. Film yourself. Also, get a mirror so you can see yourself playing in real time. All these tools will become a crucial part of your self-awareness development and sense of accountability.

Whenever you feel the tension and muscular tension accumulate and reach a point of no return, take a break, shake it off and… start again. Speed comes from being relaxed and using momentum as much as possible. 90% of my students still struggle with this and about 30% still ignore their own body language and what their muscles are telling them – which leads to no progress, overwork and frustration.

"IF YOU CAN SING IT, YOU CAN PLAY IT!"

One of my teachers told me this once, many, many moons ago, and I for sure never forgot these words. All my students have heard me "preaching" the singing praise and the reason why I do it is… because it works! Our brains agree a lot more with vocalizations of patterns, sound structures. That's why babies can learn how speak way before they can learn how to read. We are wired to memorize sounds and to refuse to do so is to waste at least 50% of your brain's ability to memorize an idea or pattern.

So to break it down: why are we constantly asked to count out loud? The answer is two-fold:

- To memorize (via vocalization) the grid/subdivision that you're working with. For example, if your exercise is in 16th notes, then you should count **1 e & ah** in order to memorize the placement of each note;

- To develop your ability to keep time. Because you're singing/vocalizing the counting, your brain is getting more and more comfortable not only with the subdivision of those rhythms but also with the distance between notes and beats.

Why should we sing drum beats/fill/rhythms? Like I said before, our brains are wired to memorize sonic patterns making it a lot faster for you to learn a new groove or fill if you vocalize what you're trying to learn to only then you should focus on teaching your limbs to execute that sound. Exactly like learning a language, you have to memorize sounds before attempting to put sentences together. This method applies to learning drum beats, fills and you should also use to develop your sight-reading, dynamics, articulation, expression, everything. Remember: **Your brain is wired to learn languages through conversation, not by staring at words on a piece of paper. Why would it be different with music?**

KNOW WHY YOU'RE PRACTICING

Ah, the last point of our checklist for success. Knowing WHY to practice. More importantly, knowing WHY you're practicing WHAT you're practicing. There are a couple of things that we must take into consideration in order to answer this question correctly.

1) Your goals;

2) Your needs;

3) Your weaknesses;

YOUR GOALS – You must define goals – no goals? No success. And I would suggest defining short-term goals (1 week to 1 month), medium-term goals (1 month to 1 year) and long-term goals (1 to 5 years). Practicing what you defined as personal goal will be a clear way of always keeping track of the "why" you're putting so much time into practice.

YOUR NEEDS – If you're in a band you'll have to learn songs, transcribe tunes, work on specific sections, etc. These are your "needs" so your sense of responsibility and your work ethic is the reason behind the effort.

YOUR WEAKNESSES – This is the most difficult of all, and as we discussed before, the most important of all. Defining your weaknesses will make you more aware of your limitations which will lead to fixing them quicker, allowing you to progress and improve faster – and with a stronger foundation for not only you'll be better musician but you'll also know what kind of work needs to be done in order to solve problems and possible chinks in one's armor.

THE PYRAMID OF SELF-EVALUATION

One of the most challenging things my students have to deal with is the notion of self-evaluation. Especially since playing a musical instrument can be so subjective. How can they know when they've accomplished something? How can they if it's time to "level up" and embrace new challenges? Self-evaluation is at the essence of learning and progress. Without it, you will be lost and dependent on others.

So the question is: how can you become more independent and self-aware? I use the **Pyramid Of Self-Evaluation**. The **Pyramid Of Self-Evaluation** is most efficient when dealing with small ideas, but it can be applied to anything. It uses LANGUAGE as its foundation and it works in 4 levels.

Technique

Vocabulary

Phrasing

Speech

Let me break it down how this works. The **Pyramid Of Self-Evaluation** serves one purpose. It helps you break the learning process into smaller chunks and smaller steps towards the goal. So let's analyse each step:

Technique

This the very first step - and it has to be so! - because it lays down the foundation that will support the whole process. Technique is your ability to "say" words correctly. Your diction, if you will. This the most fundamental step of this process, not because of its creative outcome, but because if it allows you to understand the mechanics of a specific sound/exercise, allowing you to recall it and use it in a variety of contexts, tempos and dynamic levels. My advice? Practice technique until you know the pattern by heart and you have a comprehensive understanding of its mechanics and internal movements. For example, if you're learning a Paradiddle and you're trying to apply it in a creative way, then you must first understand the movements of a Paradiddle (My apologies if you're not a drummer, but please do use this example as a reference and apply it to your craft). A Paradiddle is a lot more than **Rlrr Lrll**. It has downstrokes, upstrokes and taps that need to be analysed. It has rebound strokes that need to be physically understood and studied. There's a whole "system" behind a Paradiddle that, if overlooked, will lead to a very poor execution of the exercise and, consequentially, it will end up giving you poor creative ideas. But let's say that you've been practicing the Paradiddle now for a couple of months. How do you know when to "level up"? This when "self-evaluation" becomes crucial. I personally use a very simple approach. Just ask yourself this question:

On a scale of 1 to 10, 1 being "very bad" and 10 being "excellent", how do I grade myself in regards to TECHNIQUE?

Now is the time to be honest. If you struggle to do this, do ask your teacher to help you understand the process of self-evaluation. So, if you grade yourself a 7 or more out of 10, then level up and address your **vocabulary**.

Vocabulary

First, we must define vocabulary.

> **the body of words used in a particular language.**
>
> **"a comparison of the vocabularies of different languages"** ·
>
> **the words used in a particular subject or sphere of activity or on a particular occasion:**
>
> **"the vocabulary of law"**
>
> **the body of words known to an individual person:**
>
> **"he had a wide vocabulary"**
>
> **a list of difficult or unfamiliar words with an explanation of their meanings, accompanying a piece of specialist or foreign-language text.**
>
> **a range of artistic or stylistic forms, techniques, or movements:**
>
> **"dance companies have their own vocabularies of movement"**

Ok, so what is vocabulary? Simply put, vocabulary is the "library" of words at your disposal. In music, this means small ideas - rudiments and scales are great examples of this - that you can use to build phrasing. As always, there are multiple ways to approach this but I will stick to two tools that you can use to develop your vocabulary: **orchestration** and **dynamics**.

ORCHESTRATION

First, explore different sound sources. Make sure you stick to small ideas and make sure you memorize each idea before moving on to the next one. Speed is irrelevant at this stage of your development but I would definitely focus on keeping it slow.

DYNAMICS

This is fundamental. There is nothing more boring than listening to someone with a monotone voice. It's not only boring, but distracting and meaningless. Don't get me wrong, the ideas might be good, but how you transmit them is 90% of your success or failure at communicating them. Adding contrast and volume differences to your notes is a great of adding nuance and inflexion to what you want to say. Make sure you practice this before attempting phrasing, and of course, make sure you evaluate yourself. The rule still applies: If you don't deserve at least a 7 out of 10 in VOCABULARY, **then keep working on your vocabulary before moving on to phrasing**.

Phrasing

Let's define "phrase":

PHRASE
put into a particular form of words:
"it's important to phrase the question correctly"

> synonyms:
>
> *express · put into words · put · word · style · formulate*
>
> (phrasing)
>
> <u>divide (music) into phrases in a particular way, especially in performance:</u>
>
> "original phrasing brought out unexpected aspects of the music"

In (very) simple terms, a phrase (or sentence) is a group of words. In musical terms, we will work on combinations of ideas in order to develop meaning and purpose. You see, to have vocabulary is great, but it doesn't really mean anything unless you create coherent ideas with it. You might know some great "words", but unless you use them in context, then they might still be the **wrong** words. Combinations and context are at the essence of developing phrasing.

Start simple: two or three ideas (maximum) will suffice. Combine them, explore different configurations, different textures, different musical contexts. The more you challenge yourself, the better. The goal: to become fluent while using the words you learnt so far.

Speech

Speech. This is the holy grail. The ultimate goal. And it's also the one thing that you don't really practice. Speech is the result of all the foundational work. You learn your words, you understand your grammar, develop your phrasing skills... and after all that you apply it. That's when speech occurs. The best way to develop speech is to combine phrases and develop context. In other words: apply all those ideas you've been working on and play along to songs, play with other musicians and constantly select and tweak which ideas work where. Remember, there's no point in knowing great words unless you can use them in context and with certainty.

SUMMARY

If you're gonna take something from this chapter, then let it be this: **evaluate yourself at all times**. To make it easier - and more efficient - chunk your practice into smaller elements: technique, vocabulary, phrasing and speech. That way you can keep track of where you are and how you are doing as you keep progressing up the pyramid. And remember: Learning is NOT a race. Don't rush through practice just so you can convince yourself that you've accomplished something. There's a big difference between being busy and being productive. Stay focused and stay honest.

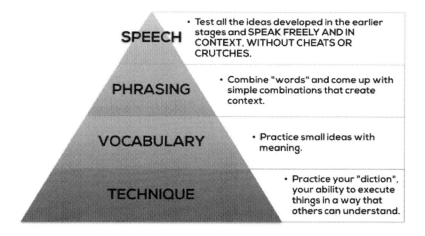

ACCOUNTABILITY

How can you improve and progress if you don't hold yourself accountable for what you're doing when you're studying and practicing? Accountability is a great skill to have and the sense of responsibility that comes with it will help you achieve everything you've planned beforehand. One of the main ways to be accountable for your practice is to keep a practice diary. In this diary you'll keep track of what you're working on, when and most importantly, HOW it went on a given day. This comments section is what's going to give you the much needed feedback that you'll go back to every time you sit down to practice. Below is an example:

MAIN FOCUS: Bass drum technique and phrasing

DATE	WHAT	TEMPO	COMMENTS
July 27th 7.28pm	Syncopation Book, page 12 with bass drum	62/97bpm	The phrasing is solid but I need to work on my stamina, calf gets tired really quick when playing heel down.
July 27th 9.15pm	Future Sounds – Permutation #5	87bpm	Number 1 to 6 are alright but I need to develop a better touch. Still not grooving.
July 28th 11.07am	Future Sounds – Permutation #5	65/75bpm	Slower tempos were better but still not flowing. Also bass drum is inconsistent when it comes to the phrasing.

This example is a perfect demonstration of objective criticism with focus on what needs to be developed. This will not only be a great way of keeping track of your progress and struggles but it will be an excellent way of exercising of your self-awareness and self-criticism. We'll address the importance of meta-cognition further into this book for now I'll finish this chapter with these words:

"The unreflected life is not worth living"

Socrates

"Learning without thought is labour lost. Thought without learning is perilous."

Confucius

REPETITIO EST MATER STUDIORUM[2]

Literally every single music teacher on earth will tell you that you have to repeat an exercise countless times before you can claim that you know it. But the big question again has to be: why? Why do we have to keep repeating the same bar over and over again? Well… have you ever heard of muscle memory?

MUSCLE MEMORY – WHAT IS IT?

Well, it might sound obvious, but… your muscles can't memorize anything. Your brain does. Muscle memory is just a common name for what I call **procedural memories**[3]. So what we're memorizing is the motor functions necessary to execute a certain exercise. Ultimately, playing a Paradiddle or a C Major scale on a piano is no different than walking or driving. Right? Almost.

In its generic form, walking and playing a rudiment is indeed the same to our brains. But we need to make a distinction between **gross motor functions** and **fine motor functions**.

GROSS MOTOR FUNCTIONS - Gross motor skills are larger movements that you make with your arms, legs, feet, or your entire body even. Crawling, running and jumping are gross motor skills.

---

[2] Repetition is the mother of learning.

[3] **Procedural memory** is a part of the long-term **memory** that is responsible for knowing how to do things, also known as motor skills. As the name implies, **procedural memory** stores information on how to perform certain procedures, such as walking, speaking, driving and… playing a paradiddle!

FINE MOTOR SKILLS – these are smaller actions. Anything that you do using your fingers, toes and hands (for example) are fine motor skills.

The main focus when it comes to acquiring muscle memory is to start SLOW. And I mean **slow**. And the reason is, again, very simple: remember when you started walking? Probably not but I can guarantee you that you didn't start by walking. You started by being on your stomach just working on keeping your head up. Then you tried to start crawling (that can be hilarious to watch by the way!) and finally... walking! But it didn't go well straight away. You fell, you got frustrated. But hey, let's backtrack... you started by just being on your stomach, you raised your head and kept it up for as long as 5 seconds. Isn't that (excuse the pun) taking it one step at a time? So why do you try to play more than what your body knows or is comfortable with? So many times I see students trying too much, too fast, too soon. Muscle memory is best developed when you respect these two rules: Rule #1 is to practice your fast movements slowly. This means that you'll practice all those motor functions that you need to play fast but it slow-motion. **High speed and low frequency**[4]. Rule #2 is to repeat those motions at least 5 minutes at a time, at the same tempo, and EXTREMELY focused on every single part of the movement you're trying to master. I'll address the subject of "speed" in detail in the next chapter.

---

[4] Speed can be thought of as the rate at which an object covers distance. A fast-moving object has a high speed and covers a relatively large distance in a short amount of time. This will be the speed of your movements – how fast you go from point A to B.

Frequency is the rate at which something occurs over a particular period of time. In this case we're referring to the space between your strokes. High frequency means fast tempo, low frequency, slow tempo.

MECHANICS VS INTENTION

Back to being self-aware and objective. Let's imagine this scenario: you're practicing your double strokes. You were told to use your wrists, let the sticks bounce, support the second stroke with your fingers and to be relaxed... Oh, you were also told that both notes need to sound even in volume and that the rhythm/frequency of your strokes needs to be consistent. This sounds... difficult. And that's because it is. It's difficult because you're either trying to focus on too many mechanical elements at a time or because you're not adapting those mechanics to the intention. Usually beginners struggle with the former and players tend to struggle with the latter – which is why they're still intermediate players...

So first you need to define the intention: are you working on controlling the bounce of the stick? Are you working on the dynamic evenness? Or are you working on speed/frequency? You need to focus on the intention and only then you can choose/select what mechanical elements need to be addressed and fixed if needed be. One of the main issues that students deal with is the fact that they try to play fast exercises using a "slow" technique. In other words, these students are careless when it comes to choosing the right mechanics for that intention (playing fast). If you want fast, you can't move your hands/fingers/wrists/forearms (or whichever parts of your body you need to utilize during that exercise) slowly and, dare I say, **lazily**. The correlation between distance that you cover, the speed of your movements and the frequency of your events if pretty much direct. Let's start by analyzing frequency and distance:

So as you can see, as the tempo increases, the distance between your starting point and the impact point needs to decrease so you can perform faster without stressing your muscles. Bear in mind however that this concept is true regardless of how high or low your starting point is. It's very important that you start with slow tempos and long distances in order to get your muscles used to movement and motor function before having to streamline it. If you practice short motions at slow tempos, those motions will still "shrink" as the tempo increases making it very difficult for you to move freely and in a relaxed fashion.

WHAT SPEED REALLY IS

Okay, so everyone wants to be fast. What most musicians don't seem to understand is how our bodies work. Speed can't be forced and it must be, slowly, cultivated. Performing music relies heavily on small muscles and, as light as they are, they might not be the fastest. So why do some musicians play so fast and yet, here we are trying to play 16th notes at 120bpm? The answer is in how you practice speed and what muscles you should be focused on. Keyword here is **HOW**.

Let's talk about fast-twitching muscles. After all, these are the solution for your speed problems.

Fast-twitch muscles break down into two categories: moderate fast-twitch (type IIA) and fast-twitch (type IIB or IIX). Moderate fast-twitch muscles are thicker, quicker to contract, and wear out more rapidly than slow-twitch. Fast-twitch, the most powerful and lowest in endurance, are activated when the body nears maximum exertion.

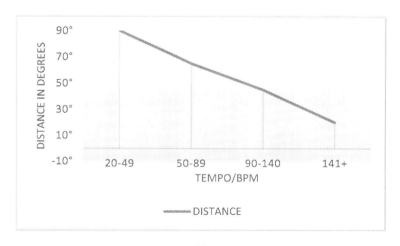

So how can you access these fast-twitching muscles? Exercise helps a lot – lifting weights, wrist/finger exercises, stretching and tension/release exercises, etc.) and of course, we can exercise these muscles also when playing. All muscles groups are essential to achieve high tempos but your body needs to learn how to move quickly. So here's my take on speed and how to access the "fast twitching":

- Speed/Velocity
- Frequency
- Motion/Direction
- Recovery
- Bursts

It is however fundamental that you understand the technique and mechanics behind each exercise. If you ignore the ideal movement that will produce the ideal result... game over. What does that mean? If you play tense, or your elbows are pointing out, or your shoulders are as high as they can be, then your end result is being blocked by all these obstacles. You might be practice the **RIGHT** exercises but what does it matter if you practicing them the **WRONG** way? Memorize this one:

What does wrong sound when played fast?

It sounds like you shouldn't get the gig.

PRACTICE THE FAST TECHNIQUES SLOWLY

In order to memorize those movements and to achieve that speed that you want to achieve, you'll have to practice those motor functions slowly. What a lot of students is that they practice the slow technique slow and they try to use that same technique when play fast. **BIG MISTAKE!** What you have to do is practice the fast techniques slowly. You have to bring the frequency (BPM) down and space your notes apart enough for you to be able to analyze and learn each motion but you have to keep the speed/velocity of your movements quite high. What you'll be developing is your twitching

33

ability, your reflexes and your "resetting" skills. Remember, it's as important to move from A to B fast as it is to recover back from B to A. Take too long to recover and you won't be able to repeat that event fast enough. And speed is nothing but the execution of a series of events that are incredibly close to each other, leaving you with very little time to recover and start again.

4 KINDS OF LEARNER

HOW TO FIND OUT WHICH ONE YOU ARE

There are three kinds of students and three fundamental ways of learning music:

- Aural learners

- Visual learners

- Read-Write learner

- Kinesthetic learners

This doesn't mean that each student only has ONE way of learning and I know that we all can learn using any of these methods. However, there's usually one that is a **TRIGGER** for absorption and understanding.

For you to find out what way works best for you, you'll have to… try them all. That's right. You can't know what you don't know and if you opt to only rely on, say, visual learning, you might be missing out on a much better and more efficient way of learning and memorizing what you're trying to learn.

Aural learners are those students who learn "by ear". Once again, this doesn't mean that this the one way these students learn but listening is fundamental to their learning experience. These students are characterized by:

- They speak slowly and tend to be natural listeners.

- They think in a linear manner.

- They prefer to have things explained to them verbally rather than to read written information.

- They learn by listening and verbalizing.

Visual learners learn mainly via observation and visualization. Usually characterized by:

35

- They tend to be fast talkers.

- They exhibit impatience and have a tendency to interrupt.

- They use words and phrases that evoke visual images.

- They learn by seeing and visualizing.

Read-write learners prefer to read information, they prefer to take their time processing it and they see taking notes as fundamental to reinforce what's being studied.

- They prefer for information to be displayed in writing, such as lists of ideas.

- They emphasize text-based input and output.

- They enjoy reading and writing in all forms.

Kinesthetic learners are doers. They belong to a category of people who prefers to try and explore their own limitations by trial and error and then analyze what they need to tweak in order to improve.

- They tend to be the slowest talkers of all.

- They tend to be slow to make decisions.

- They use all their senses to engage in learning.

- They learn by doing and solving real-life problems.

- They like hands-on approaches to things and learn through trial and error.

I would strongly advise you to find what method works best for you and what the trigger that accelerates your learning experience is.

WHOLE-BRAIN LEARNING

PRACTICE WITH AND WITHOUT AN INSTRUMENT

Excuse number one in the book: *"I didn't practice because I was away all week."* To which I reply: *"And you left your body at home?..."*

What this excuse reveals is that this student doesn't know how to practice without his/her instrument. To practice with your whole brain and your whole body is a FUNDAMENTAL part of your learning experience.

METACOGNITION

The definition of metacognition is very simple: it's the awareness and understanding of one's own thought processes. We will address self-awareness more in depth in a couple of pages but for now, let's talk about how you can wire yourself to be more aware of what you're learning, what your struggles are and how you can teach yourself to learn.

In other words, we're talking about thinking about thinking. That's right, that's not a typo. In order to learn fully, you'll have to develop metacognitive skills – the ability to learn about learning, to think about thinking and – more importantly – to self-regulate and self-critique. How can you improve if you can't even point out what needs to be improved? Sure, your teacher is there to do that. But what happens when you go home? What happens when you're in the practice room? If you can't judge, analyze and think objectively about what you're working on, then trust me, you will not improve and all you'll do is scratch the surface of everything you're trying to learn.

I always tell my students: "Never forget the difference between *getting it* and ***KNOWING IT!***". They often look at me confused. But you won't. You get it. But do you **know** it?

So here's what you need to focus on when you practice:

- ACQUIRE KNOWLEDGE – Repeat the same process until you "get it";

- RETAIN KNOWLEDGE – Don't just spew it, **speak it;**

- TRANSFER KNOWLEDGE – Get creative with the material and test how far you can go with the one piece of new information that you now **KNOW.**

So here are some of the meta-cognitive strategies that I personally use in my lessons – and that you should use during your practice time:

- Goal setting

- Constant monitoring

- Identifying what the student knows

- Identifying what the student doesn't know

- Adapting as needed.

Be strict about your goals but be flexible about how you get there.

Here's what you should be doing during your practice sessions:

- Goal setting;

- Ask yourself questions, such as:

  ○ How did it go?

  ○ How did I feel playing that exercise

  ○ Are all the different components of this exercises mastered?

- o Is this recordable? Could I perform this live, in front of an audience?

- Identify what still needs to be improved;

- Keep a practice log – writing down what you've achieved and what you still need to practice is a great metacognitive tool.

VISUALIZATION

This is the one that people struggle with the most – especially as we grow older. Basically, you have to imagine that you're practicing. Doesn't that sound appealing? Well, learning using visualization can be a great complement to your actual physical practice. This is not (yet) phantom practice but rather utilizing your imagination to create a mental image of what you want to achieve. That can be a technique, an exercise, seeing you playing in front a thousands of people, etc… In simple terms: you're using your imagination. So how exactly can you do that?

I call it **VISUAL MEDITATION**. Imagine that you're on the road – on a bus, train, plane, (but definitely NOT driving!) and you can't practice. Think again (pun intended). Close your eyes and imagine that you are practicing. See yourself in your practice room surrounded by everything you have in it. Then imagine yourself playing your instrument. Maybe even start by warming up. Then imagine yourself going through your practice diary and pick an exercise to practice. Now… practice. This might sound weird and on the verge of crazy, but it works. Give it a try!

PHANTOM PRACTICE

Phantom practice is, in a way, residual practice. Ok, that didn't help clarifying what it is. Simply put, phantom practice is your brain's ability to keep processing information even when you're not practicing. As you can imagine, how long and how efficiently you practice will directly influence how much phantom practice you'll experience. For example: if you practice 30 minutes a day, it's very likely that not much phantom practice will occur since you're brain wasn't stimulated enough. On the other hand, if you practice for 5 hours a day – on a daily basis – it's very likely that your brain will stay on "practice mode" even if you go on holidays for a week. Many of us have experienced coming back from a trip or a weekend of no practice and see and feel improvement and progress. That's why I call it **residual practice**.

There is yet another common phenomenon that might occur during "non-practice" time: you ear and sense of time gets better. You might be developing mental/brain skills that will directly affect and improve your instrumental skills.

So once again, to think about music, rhythm, melody, harmony, movements and motions, posture, and whatever else you consider during your practice time, will improve your overall skills when you're in "non-practice" time. Keep your brain alive, and your body will follow.

SELF-AWARENESS AND HONESTY

Last chapter. And this is the toughest one for me. Tough to write, tough to teach, tough to not let my own honesty take over and overpower the clarity of my explanations and thoughts. Isn't that what self-awareness is for?

I've been pushing this agenda lately and a lot of my students have been struggling quite a lot with this new approach to learning. The reason why they struggle is pretty simple: it's difficult to be honest and it's even more difficult to ask yourself the right questions. To increase your self-awareness, you'll have to make a very serious decision: how bad do you want it? How bad do you want to become that great musician that you always wanted to be? Now that you're getting close, are you willing to power through the tough times and

40

focus on what you need to improve in order to reduce the dents in your armor? This might be the most important question you could ask yourself, so I will repeat it:

How bad do you want IT?

It's not easy and it takes practice but self-awareness and honesty (even if sometimes brutal) is the secret behind your success – or lack of. To develop those skills you'll have to commit to them and under no circumstances you will shift your focus towards anything but your thoughts and actions and how these affect your reality. Your performance, your confidence, your objectivity and your own sense of realization will increase exponentially in relation to your self-awareness and, of course, awareness of your surroundings.

As mentioned before, in order to improve your self-awareness, you'll need to start asking questions. For example, if you constantly rush your phrasing, you need to ask yourself "why does that happen?" and/or "what am I thinking about/what am I feeling that makes me rush every time?". You might find out that there's a trigger behind that phenomenon of rushing. Find out what it is and you'll feel the results almost immediately.

Self-awareness – and being EXTREMELY honest about what you're aware of – is the one route towards success and self-realization. Fail to be self-aware and you'll begin to believe your own lies and your own "convenient perception of reality". How many of us have said things like:

- I don't like to practice with the metronome, it makes me play worse;

- I don't like to count out loud, it makes me play worse;

- I don't like to read, it makes me play worse;

- I don't like to record myself, makes me sound/look worse;

Surprise, surprise… none of these things makes you play worse. They only EXPOSE what was already wrong in the first place and to deprive yourself from these tools is to deprive yourself from improving.

Remember: **ask the wrong questions and you'll get the wrong answers. Ask no questions and you shall get no answers.**

From a teacher's standpoint, there's no easy way for me to teach self-awareness. I believe that in can be taught, I believe that it can be learnt. However, I also believe that you have to **want** it. You have to want to know more about yourself. You have to want it really bad for this might be most difficult challenge you'll ever face. But believe me when I say this: nothing will ever be the same again once you understand what's holding you back.

I must warn you however; do not confuse self-awareness with not taking anyone else's feedback as valid or useful. Being self-aware doesn't mean that you'll close yourself in a glass box and become an intellectual hermit. It only means that you'll take what you receive from your surroundings and analyze it until you (and I mean YOU) understand what it means in context and what it means to you in relation to your belief system and your ambitions. For example: if you're having a music lesson and your teacher says "be careful, you tend to rush those 16th notes on bar 27" then you must do two things:

- Analyze what that means in context. Go back to bar 27, play it exactly as you've been playing it and see if anything changed. Ask for feedback again. If the same result occurred, then you must move on to step two:

- Reflect and ask about how you can improve it. Is it just a matter of repetition? Probably not. Are you playing it too fast? Are you unsure of what the phrasing is so you're trying to "survive" it? Do you feel anxious whenever you play phrases like that? This is what self-awareness and metacognition can do for you. You ask the questions and your brain – and your teacher – you'll find the answers.

Once you find those answers, then you can take action. This is also a fundamental step, for **knowledge without action is futile**. What you need to be aware of is that this new course of action follows the new guidelines that you've adopted after reflecting on the feedback that you've received from your teacher/colleagues/audience. It's crucial that you create a safe environment around yourself in which you welcome constructive criticism and you don't make those who want to help and guide you feel like they shouldn't criticize you or your behavior. Creating that safe place is the quickest way to develop self-awareness. Wisdom will be to choose the criticism that you want to keep and the criticism that you'll find useless. Finding a mentor, a coach, a teacher, someone that you can trust and rely on, is a fundamental part of this process.

You must try, at least once a day, to be the "weakest" person in the room. Only then you will understand the true meaning of learning and growing. Humility is to want to learn and to know that the struggle is only a reminder of your limitations but more importantly, is the confirmation that you've started to expand your current horizons and realm of knowledge. Fail to struggle and you will never witness growth.

WHAT IS CREATIVITY?

I ask all my students to fill out what I call the *"Table Of Standards & Expectations"*. I talk about this in my book "How Do We Learn" but, to summarize, I ask all my students to fill out a self-assessment/improvement forecast form.

So... on a Sunday afternoon, one of my students is filling in the form when suddenly he asks me:

"Creativity... what do you mean by that?" Wow. I never thought of that. It took me 10 seconds to come up with an answer, and it came out something like this:

"Creativity is the ability to express yourself freely and in context, without the use of cheats or crutches."

I must admit, I was pretty proud of how I phrased that. So proud that I wrote it down, scared that I would forget it. The more I thought about it, the more sense it seemed to make.

"Creativity is the ability to express yourself freely and in context, without the use of cheats or crutches."

Yes, I'm pretty happy about how this came out. But let's break it down, I'm not a big fan of spewing poetry just for the sake of it.

I often compare learning music to learning a language. And the same goes for being musically creative. So, with that in mind, let's isolate and understand each of the 4 parts of my definition of creativity.

EXPRESS YOURSELF FREELY

Do you leave your house in the morning with a prepared speech that has **EVERYTHING** you'll say on that day? Do you know exactly what every single interaction will go like? No. But do you go mute when you're asked if you want milk in your coffee, even if you're usually never asked that question? No. That's because the amount of vocabulary you have and your knowledge of language is more than sufficient to manage unpredictability. That means that you're not **stuck** and you are able to **freely** move and adjust as conversations develop. So, why would it be any different when you play your musical instrument?

The reason why most people can't express themselves when performing is simple. Lack of what to say and lack of how to say it. Developing vocabulary is fundamental. That means understanding rhythm, melody, harmony, reading, rudiments, scales. All of it. These are your letters, words, sentences, grammar, etc... Would you be able to speak freely without these tools?

IN CONTEXT

Ok, so you got your vocabulary down. But that's not really useful unless you can listen too. And I don't just mean to listen to others, but to yourself as well, so you can assess if what you're saying is coherent and logical. I often ask my students "Why did you play that fill?", to which they (obviously) respond "I don't know... I like it?".

This is not good enough. Imagine this conversation:

- Hey João, how are you? Long time no see!
- Hey! What's up? Yeah, it's been a while!
- So tell me, what's this book you're writing about?
- Lettuce.
- What? What do you mean?
- Lettuce.
- Hmmm... okay. What about lettuce?
- Not much, I like lettuce. So I said "lettuce". Yeah.
- Right... okay, bye then.

Ok, so it's not difficult to understand that this conversation is absurd. But, am I struggling with language? No. It's context and communication that I'm butchering. I see this **everyday**. Literally everyday. Students who play random ideas, disconnected and inconsequential. Everyday. But how can we fix this?

Look, at the end of the day, you must question yourself. Always assume that you're wrong and always assume that you're not being clear enough. By doing so you will constantly get rid of all the "noise" and your speech will become more and more polished. If you're satisfied with gibberish, then your audience will be more than happy about **not engaging.**

NO CHEATS

Cheats are the worst thing you could possibly use when trying to develop creativity. Good, now that we have established that, let's understand what cheats are.

cheattʃiːt/ verb
1.act dishonestly or unfairly in order to gain an advantage.
2.avoid (something undesirable) by luck or skill.

So, are you a cheater? Let's find out. Whenever you feel like you're about to make a mistake, do you avoid it? Do you make mistakes and pretend you don't? Do you avoid working on your weaknesses? Ask yourself:

Do I cheat? Am I dishonest?

If you can answer this simple question, then you might get closer to becoming a creative mind. But don't cheat. We will all know if you do.

NO CRUTCHES

Ah... tricks. I love tricks. The problem with tricks is that they confine you in a box of limited ideas. Because you rely so much on tricks, they become a crutch, without which you can't walk... or perform. These can be little licks, little embellishments that you use. But it can also be much more than that. It can be an entire mindset that refuses to listen, explore and, **more importantly**, to avoid your tendencies. Look, we all have natural tendencies. But only by avoiding them - I'll tell you how in a minute - you will be able to get out of your comfort zone and raise your threshold of pain.

You know that thing that you never practice? Do it. Now.

First, do what you always do. Let's use drumming as an example - but do apply these ideas to whatever you do. Play by yourself (no songs) for 5 minutes. Then, write down what your tendencies are. Do you always use the same fill? Do you always default back to a specific idea? If so, write it down. That's your new rule: DO NOT PLAY THAT IDEA. EVER. Start again, play for 5 minutes. Repeat the process.

Keeping a tendencies journal is a great source of self-awareness and self-improvement. Film yourself, write daily reports on your creative progress. Always go for more, always chase the new, the unexplored, the uncomfortable.

"Creativity is the ability to express yourself freely and in context, without the use of cheats or crutches."

TO SUM UP...

Practice is a very important part of the process but as I'm sure you understand by now, just playing your instrument will not be enough. It's how you prepare your practice sessions, how you approach them and more importantly, how you wire your brain to be successful.

Now, I must be honest: it's up to you to make the right decision. You can either continue to "fake" practice or you can start taking practice and your journey of self-improvement seriously. The decision, ultimately, is yours. But so is the responsibility that comes with that decision. You want to be a pro? Then behave like one. You're planting seeds. But the size of your harvest will depend on the quality (and not just the quantity) of those seeds.

If you begin your journey at the end of it, you can only walk backwards. Start at the beginning and you shall progress everyday.

If you can't find the reason why you're struggling, it means the reason is you.

You can't lose at something that you're not supposed to win.

FOR TEACHERS ONLY

Teachers, stop trying to teach your students and start teaching them how to learn. 90% of the music teachers I know – and who taught me! – were so focused on teaching the material they had prepared for each lesson that they wouldn't even focus on what was the most important piece of that puzzle: ME! So ask yourselves: am I teaching THIS student in front of me or am I teaching my past-self? Am I teaching according to how I learn or according to how this student learns?

Have you asked your students how they feel when you teach them? Have you tried to find the most efficient way to help them? Before assuming that your students are lazy, they're not committed enough or that they don't like you, ask yourself this question: how do they learn?

THE POWER OF LETTING THEM ASK QUESTIONS

As teachers, we love to ask questions to our students, don't we? Well, as much as I get the appeal – after all, we LOVE to hear ourselves speak don't we? – but what's really going to make a difference is letting THEM ask the questions. As I always tell my students:

"There are no silly questions, only silly answers."

It's your job – yes, this right here is what your job is – to welcome all kinds of questions. Promote an inquisitive environment and let curiosity take over. It doesn't matter if your students ask you so many questions that it feels like they're disrupting the flow of your lesson. Because, guess what? This isn't YOUR lesson. This is THEIR lesson.

49

THE POWER OF ASKING THEM TO DO THE WORK

No, I'm not referring to child labor. I'm referring to promoting an atmosphere of accountability and responsibility. Have them write down what their weaknesses are and what THEY should do about it. You'll find that, of course, that is easier said than done and they will ask for your help. But now, they're not asking for you do it for them – as they usually do – but instead, they're asking for you to tell them how they can know what they should do. Below is an example – feel free to use it! – of what I give my students every month. I called it a **"Table of Expectations and Standards"**.

Table Of Expectations & Standards

Below you'll find a series of expectations and different fields of study. Here's how it works:

WHAT WILL YOU DO – This is where you describe exactly what you will practice in order to improve this field;

HOW IMPORTANT IS IT? – Rate how important it is to you to address these fields/weaknesses (0=meaningless, 10=very important);

HOW ARE YOU DOING? – rate how successful you were in the last month (0=not successful at all, 10=very successful)

WHAT SHOULD YOU ADDRESS FIRST? – This is where you number each field by how urgent it is for you to start practicing (1=Very urgent, 8=not urgent at all)

Be honest, only when facing your weaknesses you'll be able to find your strengths.

FIELD/ISSUE	WHAT WILL YOU DO?	HOW IMPORTANT IS IT?	HOW ARE YOU DOING?	WHAT SHOULD YOU ADDRESS FIRST?
Technique				
Time-Keeping				
Reading				
Phrasing/Fills				
Dynamics				
Independence				
Versatility				
Creativity				

This "little" (but very challenging) exercise transfers the responsibility to your students and it will teach them a very valuable lesson: no one can know what they SHOULD be doing better than themselves. This is the beginning of their metacognitive journey.

WHY DO I HAVE SO MANY "SAYINGS"?

This is something that my students will find hilarious – or just weird, we'll see… - but they know that I have all these sayings, metaphors and analogies. Here's the secret behind all those expressions: I use them as triggers and as a way of programming their brains faster. Using repetitive sayings is one of the easiest and most efficient ways of programming someone's brain. This is known as NLP, or neuro-linguistic programming[5]. This works so well that often I just need to point to a certain part of my face to create with necessary reaction or change from the student. They already know that when I point at my chin, it means "count out loud". So these triggers allow for more efficient communication and, more importantly, it allows for more lasting understanding and absorption of concepts – including emotional states of mind. Developing skills in this area will be extremely useful for when you're dealing with students who might have trouble leaving certain states of mind which could be holding them back – for example: lack of confidence, lack of focus or even just a lot of nervous energy which can lead to rushing their phrasing. Remember: it's ALL in the brain. Their limbs have nothing to do with it. So here are my favorite and most used sayings:

- **There are no silly questions, only silly answers;**

- **If you're not struggling, you're not doing it right;**

- **Don't TRY to be smart. Just BE smart;**

- **Nothing is unfixable unless YOU don't fix it;**

---

[5] From www.nlpu.com: NLP is a **pragmatic school of thought** - an 'epistemology' - that addresses the many levels involved in being human. NLP is a multi-dimensional process that involves the development of behavioral competence and flexibility, but also involves strategic thinking and an understanding of the mental and cognitive processes behind behavior. NLP provides tools and skills for the development of states of individual excellence, but it also establishes a system of empowering beliefs and presuppositions about what human beings are, what communication is and what the process of change is all about. At another level, NLP is about self-discovery, exploring identity and mission. It also provides a framework for understanding and relating to the 'spiritual' part of human experience that reaches beyond us as individuals to our family, community and global systems. NLP is not only about competence and excellence, it is about wisdom and vision.

- **Be strict with your goals but be flexible with how you get there;**

- **It's never WHAT you practice but HOW you practice;**

- **You can't know what you don't know.**

As I'm sure you can tell, many of these are focused on building a strong sense of "you" (you being the student), once again transferring the responsibility to them. But these phrases also focus on the concept of **empowered practice**, which basically means that the students will not only feel responsible and accountable for their practice but they will also know when to celebrate their victories.

It's not your job to make it easy. Your job is to make it SIMPLE. Students will always need your guidance as long as you focus on breakdown the mechanics and processes behind the results. To not just show them the goal but make sure you show them the way to get there. And once you do that, let them walk and become an observer.

FOR PARENTS ONLY

Be the parent you want your child to become.

This can be quite a difficult chapter too... as a parent myself, it's always difficult to be told how to raise our kids, how to be a better parent and how to help our children grow to be more complete and fulfilled. The problem is that we often care too much and protect our children too much, depriving them from developing problem-solving skills, the ability to be critical of themselves and growing self-awareness. So, the real question is: **what can we, as parents, do to support our kids during this difficult journey that is learning a musical instrument?** Here's a list of things to consider (and commit to!):

- **Be on time/attend your lessons** – sounds obvious right? But often students "forget" they had a lesson (what about their parents? Did they also forget?) and end up missing countless lessons a year. Also, students who tend to get to their lessons consistently late are often the ones who barely progress. Coincidence?

- **Know what their homework is** – often parents "forget" to ask their children what their homework is – you probably assume that there's no homework? – and let their children "off the hook". Once again, coincidence or not, these are the students usually show signs of slow or no progress at all.

- **Make sure you create a practice routine** – children need guidance and rules and practice time will not "just happen". Sure, we want them to have fun and enjoy the experience, but do you actually believe that your son/daughter will enjoy the experience of learning an instrument when they never get better at it? Not practicing is not "making it more enjoyable", but rather a recipe for frustration and eventually, to give up. If putting in the work becomes a chore instead of a challenge, then students will end up memorizing this behavioral pattern and react the same way every time they face a challenge: **they'll give up.**

- **Be supportive of them, even when they seem to struggle** – I know this sounds ridiculous, but I have met parents who don't really care if they're kids are struggling to learn their instrument – or even worse, mock them and make them look incapable of learning. Please, do not do this. Learning a musical instrument is incredibly difficult as it is, don't assume that it's your kid's fault.

- **Ask questions!** – Why not? I give my students reports on their progress, why don't you ask the teacher how your kid is doing, what you can do to help him/her progress quicker and better, ask everything! If you show interest and curiosity, your child will grow to be curious and interested.

- **Participate but don't disrupt** – Yes, parent participation is extremely important, but it can become "too much". Avoid taking over the lesson and, if possible, don't attend the lesson and instead, watch the last 5 minutes of your child's lesson to see if there was any improvement, what was taught and ask his/her teacher questions regarding the lessons.

- **Commitment is forever** – Your child will want to give up at times. It's called feeling challenged, feeling scared of failing and sometimes, just laziness. It happens and we all know what the price of indulgence can be. Teach your children to overcome those moments, remind them that commitment always pays off and that everything will be challenging but the feeling that they'll get when they achieve will be the well-deserved reward.

Music, as an academic subject, is very important at any stage of your kid's cognitive development and the main reason why a lot of students give up their lessons is because many parents don't see learning music is not as important as math, history or geography. I might be biased, but music is as (if not more) important than most subjects that children study in schools these days. If you tell your kid "it's okay if you fail Math and English this year" or "you don't have to go to school anymore", do you think your kids will make the "right thing"? No. They will IMMEDIATELY make a conscious decision of never studying again. So guess what happens when you tell them that they don't have to go to music lessons if they don't want or that they don't have to practice since it's just a hobby? They will quit, that's what.

BONUS MATERIAL

CASE STUDIES

Sometimes all we need is to see ourselves reflected on other people, allowing us to identify our own flaws and qualities. The following case studies are real, but of course, the names are not. These are just some of the worst and best case scenarios when it comes to teacher/student relationships.

The Delusional Student...

This "story" will probably be mashup of many students who I've taught over the last decade. I wish I could say that I've only had one student who had delusions of grandeur but that wouldn't be true. This is just one of those stories.

Calvin S. (not a real name) is a 17 year old student who wants to pursue a career in music. The problem is, Calvin is not a great drummer. Calvin isn't a great student either. Calvin has really bad habits that he doesn't seem to want to correct. He was my student for over 2 years and unfortunately, Calvin couldn't cope with the idea of self-improvement. He really, REALLY wanted to become a professional musician but he wasn't emotionally ready to deal with his own weaknesses and blind spots. It was always very difficult and challenging to teach Calvin, but the reasons might surprise you. There are mainly two:

- *Calvin NEVER brought his material and books to his lessons. He seemed to be adamant on not following up on any of the material that we worked on our lessons, including technical exercises that were meant to help him with his bass drum technique – by far his biggest weakness alongside with his musical ideas and execution;*

- *Calvin saw himself as a very good drummer.*

As you can imagine, there's a major issue here. Because this student never really saw his own flaws as a problem, he ended being stuck in this mindset, this frame of mind that got him used to his weaknesses and with that comes… delusion.

PS: Calvin is still not a professional musician.

The Sleepy Student

This case study will prove one thing: not even the best teacher in the world can change lack of will. Will J. is a 12 year old student who started playing when he was 8 and started studying with me when he was 10 years old. There are two problems with this student: his passion (or lack of) and his parents. Yes, we're going there. Parents, sit tight. This is going to be a rough ride.

Will is… lazy. And I don't use that word when I don't mean it. Sure, all teens are a bit lazy but Will just lacks energy. Mental and physical energy. Now, I must clarify something: he's an active kid, he has no physical conditions that make him struggle. He does sports, he goes to school, the whole nine yards. But in my classroom? No. Nothing. No energy, no will, no passion, no effort.

Why? Because Will — and I apologize if it sounds harsh — doesn't care. But the most important question is: why doesn't he care? The answer is as important as it is difficult. **Will is allowed to not care.**

Will's parents allow him to be lazy. They allow him to not take music seriously. They don't expect him to practice, they don't request results or promote any kind of accountability. And that is exactly why Will has been asked to stop his lessons with me.

The Student Who's (Almost) Always Depressed

This is difficult to deal with but it's VERY important that teachers know how to handle students who struggle with motivation. There is a fundamental difference between students who struggle and students who lack motivation. The latter depress. My job, as an educator, is to find out why the student feels so low and then come up with a plan that will allow him or her to find the missing motivation that will start the learning process. I had a student back in 2012 that constantly cried. That's right. Sometimes all it took was asking "Did you practice this week?". Tears.

Messien (again, not a real name but he is French so I gave him a French name) is a sweet, delicate 11-year-old child. However, when under pressure, Messien would always crack. It took me 9 months to find out why. Messien was always worried that he would fail. So he would just give up before even allowing himself to fail. I told him the following: "Look. I understand that you're scared of making mistakes. I understand that you feel that the stakes are high and maybe I gave you the wrong impression. I don't expect you to be perfect. I only want you to experience how amazing it is to succeed at something. And you can't succeed at anything in life if you don't try and more importantly, if you're not okay with the idea of making mistakes. Mistakes are just reminders. They remind you that you're not there yet. Failures? You can only fail if you give up. Make a mistake, learn and try something different and you'll be a champion in my book". Messien smiled (for the first time) and said "But my parents don't want me to practice.", to which I replied "I struggle to believe that, what do you mean by that?". His reply answered all my questions. "They don't like how I play."

Needless to say, I had a little chat with Messien's parents. The result? They canceled his lessons with me. I still think about this student and I do feel that I failed for I failed to see what the problem was earlier and I feel that I allowed it to last for far too long. His parents were very critical and dismissive of him and unfortunately I failed to create a culture of tolerance, respect and acceptance. We grow and learn and nowadays I don't let anyone give up before they try. Everyone struggles. We just need to learn to embrace that fact.

The "Perfect" Student

Some students just have the whole package. They're focused, they're positive, they're disciplined, they're willing to listen and be criticized, they crave guidance and they have a creative and independent mind. This is, of course, a rare breed. I'm lucky enough to have met a couple of students like this and that I managed to help a couple of students to become very passionate and efficient students. Because this case study is a positive one, I will be using the student's real name.

Connor Crossland has been my student since 2015. When I met Connor he was already a talented drummer but with a lot of dents on his armor. But the thing that made Connor special was that he knew that, he wanted to fix them and he wanted to learn more every day. He always gets excited when learning new exercises or whenever I showed him new ideas.

Connor is now studying music performance at a highly-respected college/university in Manchester, England. And he's still my private student. I'm so proud of you dude. Remember, do it right and the keys are yours.

Ok, let me break it down for you: how can you become the "perfect" student (and eventually the perfect professional)? A quick warning: this might be the most important thing I write in this book.

All these traits of personality are, in my opinion, crucial if you wish to achieve success, both in music, in business and in life. Needless to say, these are, of course, some of the traits of an EXCELLENT student. If you focus on developing – and keeping – these traits of personality and professionalism, you will increase your odds of succeeding. Connor is a walking example of all of these and he's already, at the age of 17, making money playing the drums, studying at a highly-respected music university and I know for a fact that Connor will become a **very** successful professional musician.

I WOULD LIKE TO THANK:

This book would never existed if wasn't for my students so, first and foremost, this book is for them. Also my teachers – Hugo Danin, Michael Lauren, Claus Hessler, JP Bouvet and Juan Carlito Mendoza – who made me want to be a better professional, a better musician and a better educator.

My family – both back "home" and here in the United Kingdom – play a massive role in my life for they allow me to live this crazy dream of mine.

To the companies that I endorse and support me: Soultone cymbals and Vic Firth drum sticks.

And of course, to you. May this book help you be a better student and a better teacher.

Everyone is different and everyone learns at a different pace and using different methods. This book only aims to share my methods and ask you to explore them, test them and discover which ones (if any) work for you.

Please do get in touch if you want to discuss these methods further (you can find me on facebook, twitter or send me an e-mail to admin@leedsdrumacademy.com).

I wish you all the best and I hope you achieve everything you desire. Be happy.

João Figueiredo

Printed in Great Britain
by Amazon